MAY 1 0 2016

**WOODS BRANCH
GROSSE POINTE PUBLIC LIBRARY
GROSSE POINTE, MI 48236**

SAINT POPE
JOHN PAUL II

Religious Leader and Humanitarian

SAINT POPE
JOHN PAUL II

Religious Leader and Humanitarian

BY JUDY DODGE CUMMINGS

CONTENT CONSULTANT
DR. MASSIMO FAGGIOLI
ASSISTANT PROFESSOR,
HISTORY OF MODERN CHRISTIANITY
UNIVERSITY OF SAINT THOMAS

Essential Library
An Imprint of Abdo Publishing | abdopublishing.com

abdopublishing.com

Published by Abdo Publishing, a division of ABDO, PO Box 398166, Minneapolis, Minnesota 55439. Copyright © 2016 by Abdo Consulting Group, Inc. International copyrights reserved in all countries. No part of this book may be reproduced in any form without written permission from the publisher. Essential Library™ is a trademark and logo of Abdo Publishing.

Printed in the United States of America, North Mankato, Minnesota
062015
092015

THIS BOOK CONTAINS RECYCLED MATERIALS

Cover Photo: Massimo Sambucceti/AP Images
Interior Photos: Massimo Sambucceti/AP Images, 2; Bettmann/Corbis, 6, 9, 51; AP Images, 13, 20, 24, 45, 47, 48, 55, 59, 67; STF/AFP/Getty Images, 14; Shutterstock Images, 17; Viviane Riviere/Roger Viollet/Getty Images, 22, 29, 34, 41; Mariusz S. Jurgielewicz/Shutterstock Images, 33; Laski Diffusion/Getty Images, 39; Str Old/Reuters, 56; Alex Bowie/Getty Images, 63; Wally McNamee/Corbis, 70; Marcy Nighswander/AP Images, 76; Heinz Ducklau/AP Images, 78; Ricardo Mazalan/AP Images, 80; Cliff Schiappa/AP Images, 82; Andrew Medichini/AP Images, 85; Filippo Monteforte/AP Images, 88; Czarek Sokolowski/AP Images, 90; Giuseppe Cacace/AFP/Getty Images, 94

Editor: Megan Anderson
Series Designer: Becky Daum

Library of Congress Control Number: 2015934085

Cataloging-in-Publication Data

Dodge Cummings, Judy.
 Saint Pope John Paul II: Religious leader and humanitarian / Judy Dodge Cummings.
 p. cm. -- (Essential lives)
Includes bibliographical references and index.
ISBN 978-1-62403-895-2
 1. John Paul--II,--Pope--1920-2005--Juvenile literature. 2. Popes--Biography--Juvenile literature. 3. Christian saints--Poland--Biography--Juvenile literature.
 I. Title.
282/.092--dc23
 [B]   2015934085

CONTENTS

CHAPTER 1
A SMOKY SKY 6

CHAPTER 2
SON OF POLAND 14

CHAPTER 3
FAITH FORGED BY WAR 22

CHAPTER 4
RISE THROUGH THE CHURCH 34

CHAPTER 5
A POPE FOR THE MODERN AGE 48

CHAPTER 6
CONFRONTATIONS AND VICTORY 56

CHAPTER 7
TROUBLE IN THE SECOND DECADE 70

CHAPTER 8
THE FINAL YEARS 82

Timeline	96
Essential Facts	100
Glossary	102
Additional Resources	104
Source Notes	106
Index	110
About the Author	112

CHAPTER ONE

A SMOKY SKY

Black smoke wafted from the chimney on the roof of Saint Peter's Basilica in Vatican City, Italy, on October 16, 1978. Disappointment thrummed through the crowd gathered in the square below. Black smoke was a sign. The College of Cardinals had voted, but no man had yet earned the majority needed to be elected pope.

Hundreds of millions of Catholics around the world awaited the identity of the next pope. The air in the crowd was thick with tension. The pope of the Catholic Church is one of the most powerful men in the world, guiding Catholics in countries across the globe. A papal election had been held less than two months previously, when Pope Paul VI died. The cardinals then elected Pope John Paul I, but he passed away unexpectedly after only 33 days in office.

The day grew late. The crowd in Saint Peter's Square swelled. Bodies pressed close together, and people talked excitedly in Italian. News cameras were

White smoke signals to the anxious crowd in Saint Peter's Square a new pope has been elected.

positioned close to the Vatican's central balcony. Why was the election taking so long?

The Conclave

Few in the crowd knew what was happening inside the Sistine Chapel of Saint Peter's Basilica. The conclave is a secret ceremony the church has used for centuries. The 111 cardinals inside the chapel had taken a vow of secrecy.

POPE JOHN PAUL I

Cardinal Albino Luciani died after only 33 days of serving as Pope John Paul I. He had medical problems, with his legs swelling so badly he had to wear slippers instead of shoes. He would walk on the rooftop of the Vatican to improve his circulation. One windy afternoon a stack of confidential papers flew out of John Paul I's hand while he was walking on the roof. The Vatican guards had to leap from rooftop to rooftop to collect the papers. Following the incident, John Paul I was allowed to walk only in his study. On September 29, 1978, at 5:00 a.m. a nun noticed the pope had not emerged for his morning coffee. She entered his bedroom to find John Paul I sitting up in bed, dead. The Vatican tried to disguise the fact that they had not monitored his deteriorating health. This cover-up ignited the rumor that a group of cardinals had murdered John Paul I. A full investigation was done under John Paul II. The investigation found John Paul I had not been the victim of foul play, but his medical care had been neglected.

Cardinals enter the Sistine Chapel during the 1978 papal election.

For the past two days the cardinals had lived in bare quarters. Upon entering the conclave, each cardinal was given one roll of toilet paper, two pens, and ten sheets of writing paper. The rooms where each man slept offered few comforts: a straight-backed chair, a plastic wastebasket, one small lamp, and a single bed with a narrow mattress atop wire mesh. The leaders were used to much more luxurious accommodations. However, they did not need to get too comfortable. After all, virtually every pope in the last 100 years had been elected in the first or second round of voting.

The election of 1978 would be different. In order to win the election, a man needed a two-thirds majority, but over the next 48 hours the cardinals voted seven times. Seven times the sky turned black.

A Radical Choice

The crowd outside Saint Peter's grew restless. The sun dropped below the horizon. A full moon rose above the Tiber River, and floodlights turned on. At 6:45 p.m., a cry of joy rose from the crowd. White smoke billowed from the chimney. A new pope had been selected.

VOTING FOR POPE

During a conclave, each cardinal receives a ballot with these words printed across the top: "I chose as supreme pontiff."[1] They record the name of the man they want as their next leader. After they vote, the cardinals parade down the aisle to the altar. Each man kneels, recites a prayer in Latin, and places his folded ballot on a plate. Tension mounts as the name on each ballot is read out loud. According to tradition, ballots are immediately fed into a special stove. If no man receives the majority needed to win the nomination, black smoke pours from the chimney to inform the crowd below no leader has been chosen yet. If a new pope is chosen, white smoke billows from the chimney.

All eyes were on the central balcony. The multipaned, double-glass doors swung open. A priest dressed in white robes strode out, holding a large cross in front of him. Senior Cardinal Pericle Felici followed, dressed in a red robe and skullcap and flanked by two more priests. In Latin, Cardinal Felici said, "I bring you tidings of great joy."[2] Then he announced who had been elected the new pope: Karol Wojtyla.

There was a smattering of applause from the 150,000 people jammed in the square. No one had heard of this man. American priest and writer Andrew Greely was present that day. Someone asked Greeley if the new pope was from Africa. Others thought the name Wojtyla sounded Chinese. Greeley, however, laughed and said the new pope was Polish. Even

DRESSING A NEW POPE

For five generations, the Gammarelli family in Italy has made the cassocks, or robes, for the popes. They keep a record of all the cardinals' measurements. During each papal election, they make a small, medium, and large cassock based on predictions of who will win the election, so it is ready for the new pope to wear. But no one expected Karol Wojtyla to win. Even worse, no one knew his measurements because he bought his cardinal robes secondhand. The Gammarelli's were lucky. At 5 feet, 11 inches (180 cm) tall and 170 pounds (77 kg), the medium-sized cassock fit John Paul perfectly.

the media was unprepared for Wojtyla's election. ABC News anchor Peter Jennings said, "This is quite an extraordinary surprise. To be perfectly honest, I can't even pronounce his name yet."[3]

Karol Wojtyla (voy-TIH-wa) was only 58 years old, the youngest pope in the last 132 years. Wojtyla was Polish. There had not been a non-Italian pope for 455 years, and in the 2,000-year history of the church there had never been a Polish pope.

Cardinal Felici announced Wojtyla would now be known as Pope John Paul II. The citizens of Poland celebrated, but Catholics unfamiliar with their new pope were uncertain. Who was this man? Leaders of governments in Eastern Europe knew the new pontiff well and were afraid. Pope John Paul II was their enemy, and they prepared for battle.

SPEAKING TO THE FAITHFUL

Less than an hour after being elected, John Paul II appeared on a balcony overlooking the throng in Saint Peter's Square. The mostly Italian crowd gave him a lukewarm welcome at first. They had been expecting the election of an Italian. Then John Paul began to speak, not in Polish, but in Italian. He said, "I don't know if I can make myself clear in your . . . in *our* Italian language."[4] The people cheered. Speaking the language of his audience became a trademark of Pope John Paul II, and people loved him for it.

The first Polish pope, John Paul II was considered a surprising choice for the role.

CHAPTER
TWO

SON OF POLAND

Karol Jozef Wojtyla was born on May 18, 1920, in Poland, to Karol Wojtyla Sr., a retired army officer known as "the Lieutenant," and Emilia Kaczorowska, a schoolteacher. They married in 1906 and had three children: Edmund, Olga (who died in 1914), and Karol. After Olga's death, Emilia's health began failing.

Karol grew up in Wadowice, Poland, a town of approximately 7,000 people located 30 miles (50 km) from Kraków.[1] The family lived modestly in a second-floor apartment along the town square. Their home consisted of only a living room, a kitchen that doubled as a bedroom, and a second bedroom.

Motherless Child

The spring air beckoned the children outside on April 13, 1929, but eight-year-old Karol did not play soccer with his friends. Instead a teacher delivered the

---

As it is for most Catholics, first communion was an important occasion for Karol.

news that would change his life. His mother had died from an illness related to her heart and kidneys.

Karol's father had just been at the school. He had instructed the teacher to tell young Karol that his mother had died. The teacher was prepared for the child to sob in her arms. But Karol did not cry. He simply said, "It was God's will."[2]

With Emilia's death, the family lost what Karol later described as, "the soul of home."[3] The Lieutenant took Karol to nearby Kalwaria, where there was a shrine to the Virgin Mary. For the rest of his life, Karol worshiped the Virgin Mary.

FAMILY OF FAITH

Religion was important to the Wojtyla family. There was an altar in their bedroom and a bowl of holy water near the front door. Karol used to pretend he was a priest, dressed in a white-sashed robe his mother made for him. Friends remembered Karol as deeply but quietly religious. One classmate said, "He never beat his breast or crossed himself in public for all to see."[4] Another friend used to do homework at the Wojtyla's house after school. He noticed Karol would always disappear for a few minutes after he finished an assignment. One day the friend peeked in the other room and found Karol on his knees in prayer. At age 15, Karol became leader of the Marian Sodality, a group dedicated to the worship of the Virgin Mary. To young Karol, Mary represented duty, responsibility, and certainty. In 1981, when Karol survived an assassin's bullet as pope, he was positive the Virgin Mary had protected him.

The Basilica of Offertory of Holy Mary in Wadowice was the site of Karol's baptism in June 1920.

The Lieutenant raised his son alone, cooking, cleaning, and doing all the traditional chores a mother would do. In turn, Karol respected him. The boy came home every day to share lunch with his father. Karol was a skilled athlete and played goalie on the neighborhood

> ### CHILDHOOD ACTIVITIES
>
> Growing up, Karol and his friends swam in the stream that ran through town. In the winter, town leaders iced over a tennis court, turned on lights and music, and the court became a skating rink. Sometimes the children played hockey on a nearby pond. Karol loved to hike in the mountains, even though wolves roamed the countryside.

soccer team. But as soon as the clock struck 4:00 p.m., he quit playing and went home, even in the middle of a game. His father was expecting him. After he became pope, Karol recalled his father's faith. He said, "Sometimes I would wake up during the night and find my father on his knees, just as I would always see him kneeling in the parish church."[5] This example of faith was Karol's model growing up.

In 1931, Karol began attending the local junior high. A teacher described him as "lively, very talented, very quick and very good. He had an optimistic nature."[6] Karol's brother, Edmund, had graduated from medical school and moved closer to home. The brothers went to soccer matches together.

The number of Jews living in Wadowice was unusually large. Jews made up approximately 20 to 30 percent of the town's population.[7] The town synagogue, or Jewish temple, was near Karol's school.

Anti-Semitism had a long history in Polish Christianity. Church leaders often preached against Jews from the pulpit. Jews were blamed for Jesus's death, and sometimes crowds attacked Jews after church festivities. Karol was immersed in this religious intolerance, even though he never showed any personal anti-Semitism.

At the same time, many of Karol's friends and neighbors were Jewish, including his landlord, members of his soccer team, and his best friend, Jerzy Kluger. Half a century later, when asked about the murder of millions of Polish Jews during the Holocaust, Karol's face would cloud over. Those deaths were personal for him.

Teenage Years

Tragedy struck the Wojtyla family again in 1932 when Karol was 12 years old. An outbreak of scarlet fever hit the town. Edmund doctored the victims and became infected, dying a few days later. Shortly after the funeral, a neighbor saw Karol on the street. She offered her

JERZY KLUGER

Jerzy Kluger, Karol's best friend, was Jewish. When Jerzy found out he and Karol had both passed the high school entrance exam, he ran into the Catholic church to find Karol, who was helping with the Mass. A woman looked at Jerzy in shock. She was surprised to see a Jewish boy in a Catholic church. But Karol laughed and said, "Why? Aren't we all God's children?"[8]

SAINT POPE JOHN PAUL II • 19

As a grammar school student, Karol earned top grades in religion, language, arithmetic, and singing.

sympathies and, similar to when his mother died, Karol replied, "Such was God's will."[9] Even when the world seemed bleak, faith sustained him.

Drama became Karol's creative outlet. Poland has a rich tradition of live theater. In the early 1930s, Karol met Mieczyslaw Kotlarcyzk, who ran the Amateur University Theatre in Wadowice. First, Karol began acting in school plays. Then, when he was 16, he took a professional acting job with Kotlarcyzk's productions.

Karol's charisma in front of an audience drew the attention of church officials. In 1938, Adam Sapieha, the archbishop of Kraków, came to Wadowice to speak at Karol's high school graduation. As the best orator in school, Karol gave the welcoming address. The archbishop was impressed with the boy's performance and asked if Karol intended to become a priest. Absolutely not, Karol said—he was in love with the theater.

Although Karol would eventually take the stage hundreds of times, it would not be in the way he originally envisioned. Karol would soon find himself called in a different direction.

> **POLISH PRIDE**
>
> To understand the pope Karol would become, one must understand his country. In the Middle Ages, Poland was an empire with a wealthy land-owning class, a strong military, and a distinct culture. Invasions by the Ottoman Empire in the 1600s had weakened Poland, and the country was eventually partitioned between Germany, the Austro-Hungarian Empire, and Russia. For 125 years the nation of Poland disappeared from the map of Europe. Only in 1919, after a peace treaty ended World War I (1914–1918), did Poland emerge again as an independent nation. During these lost decades, the Catholic Church preserved Poland's literature and language.

CHAPTER
THREE

FAITH FORGED BY WAR

In 1939, Karol and his father moved to Kraków, Poland's third-largest city, so Karol could study language and literature at Jagiellonian University.[1] Around this time, German troops lead by Adolf Hitler, the dictator of Germany, had defeated Austria and Czechoslovakia. In August, Hitler announced a pact with Joseph Stalin, the Communist leader of the Soviet Union. Hitler and Stalin agreed to divide the land lying between them—Poland.

In the morning on September 1, 1.5 million German soldiers invaded Poland.[2] Thousands of tanks rolled down rutty country lanes, and German bomber aircraft flew in the sky above. It was the start of World War II.

But not even war deterred Karol from his religious duties. Despite the bombing raids that morning, Karol walked to the Wawel Cathedral. As sirens screamed and

Karol moved with his father into the basement of a Kraków home owned by Karol's uncle in 1939.

The Polish people suffered greatly under German occupation.

rockets roared, he confessed his sins to Father Figelwicz at the cathedral.

Afterward, Karol returned home to fetch his father and collect a few possessions. They headed toward East Poland, away from the battlefront. Other refugees had packed the roads, with horses pulling carts filled with suitcases. But Karol and his father discovered East Poland was not any safer, so they decided to return to their home in Kraków.

By September 6, Kraków had fallen and members of the city's government fled to London in the United

Kingdom. Stalin then sent Soviet troops across Poland's border and occupied the eastern half of the country. The nation known as Poland had disappeared.

Under the Nazi Boot

Hitler wanted complete control of Poland. In order to achieve this, he would have to erase the influence of the Catholic Church. Leaders of Hitler's Nazi Party closed the Wawel Cathedral and its seminary. During the five years of Germany's occupation of Poland, 1,932 priests, 850 monks, and 289 nuns were killed.[3]

Education was another institution targeted by the Nazis, and they closed Jagiellonian University. Instead of going to school, Karol arranged a secret program of study with some language professors. Although the new academic term was supposed to begin on November 6, 1939, Nazi officials ordered all of the university's professors to gather in the Jagiellonian University auditorium. The Gestapo, the German secret police, transported all of the teachers to a concentration camp in Germany.

Nineteen-year-old Karol witnessed these injustices, shaping his lifelong social and political beliefs. He believed, as he wrote to a friend in November 1939, the true liberation of people must be through faith in Jesus Christ.

Although his university had closed, Karol continued studying on his own. He wrote to a friend, "I read, write, learn, pray and fight within myself. Sometimes I feel horrible pressure, sadness, depression, evil. Sometimes I almost glean the dawn, great lightness."[4] This time was the most creative of Karol's life. He wrote many poems and produced a three-act play based on biblical themes. He intended to become a great Polish playwright.

However, the Nazis had closed down almost all Polish theaters. One night, Halina Królikiewicz, Karol's costar from back in Wadowice, knocked on Karol's door. Królikiewicz and Karol gathered other friends and formed a secret theatrical group. If caught, Karol could have been sent to a concentration camp or executed. But keeping Polish theater alive was one way to show resistance against the enemy.

Turning Point

One cold February day in 1940, Karol's life took a new direction—one that would lead him away from drama and toward the priesthood. He went to a church near his house for a living rosary. These rosaries were prayer circles designed to connect young men to church activities. Forty-year-old Jan Tyranowski, who was leading the gathering, almost immediately became Karol's spiritual mentor. Karol later described Tyranowski as "a man of especially deep spirituality."[5]

Tyranowski and Karol meditated together and discussed the power of will over intellect. Tyranowski

THE HOLOCAUST

The Holocaust was the Nazis' systematic attempt to exterminate all European Jews during World War II. During the Holocaust, the Nazis murdered 6 million European Jews.[6] The Nazis established concentration camps where Jews were forced into labor under extreme conditions. Killing centers were also set up for the mass murder of almost 2.7 million Jews, through the use of poisonous gas or shooting squads.[7] The largest of the Nazi concentration camps was Auschwitz, which was located in Poland, approximately 37 miles (60 km) west of Kraków. Auschwitz was made up of three camps, including a killing center.

Ninety percent of Polish Jews—more than 3 million people—were killed using guns, starvation, or the gas chambers.[8] Many priests, nuns, and other Poles risked execution as they hid Jews, forged identity cards, or smuggled food into the ghetto. Karol did not. He said nothing in Poland about the brutality against the Jews until he was elected pope. The tradition of anti-Semitism in Poland bred a culture of guilt and silence that muzzled Karol. As pope, he tried to make amends for the long silence as his countrymen were massacred. In 1993, he became the first pope to authorize diplomatic relations with Israel, the Jewish country formed after World War II. With this gesture, John Paul II made it clear the long-persecuted Jews had a right to their own nation.

taught Karol, who had always valued book learning, how to be more mystical and seek the inner life of his soul, not just his mind. Tyranowski's representation of a life devoted to God was very appealing to Karol.

As Karol was expanding his spiritual experiences, German control of Poland tightened. Poles were required to have an approved job or they would be deported to a concentration camp or shot. Friends found Karol a job at a quarry. Each morning, Karol walked three miles (5 km) from his apartment to the quarry. The quarry was one mile (1.6 km) across, with cliffs dropping hundreds of feet to the ground below. Karol loaded heavy limestone into rail cars, which was backbreaking work.

During the winter of 1940–1941, the underground theater group persisted. They met each Sunday to either practice or perform. But on February 18, 1941, tragedy struck Karol again. His father had been sick since Christmas and was confined to his bed.

ACTS OF FAITH

When church bells rang during Karol's shift, he put down his buckets, crossed himself, kneeled, and prayed. Other workers gently teased him and threw things at him in jest, but Karol was not embarrassed to show his faith. He later said his friendship with his coworkers helped shape his priesthood. He grew to understand "their human work, and their dignity."[9]

While working at the quarry, Karol traded his monthly ration of cigarettes and vodka for lard in order to keep up his strength.

> ## BRUSH WITH DEATH
>
> On February 29, 1944, Karol was walking home from a double shift when a German army truck struck him from behind. A passing woman saw Karol's body lying near the road, covered in blood. The driver of a lumber truck took Karol to the hospital, where doctors diagnosed him with a brain concussion and abrasions. Karol was unconscious for nine hours, a dangerously long time, and had to remain in the hospital for two weeks.

Karol went to buy his father's medicine and pick up the dried fruit and meat patties a friend had prepared for dinner. When he returned home, Karol discovered his father sprawled across his bed. He had died from either a heart attack or stroke. Karol was not yet 21.

Following the death of his father, Karol moved in with friends. He was distraught, and his friends worried. He visited a church across the street daily to pray. Some historians later compared Karol to the nation of Poland—loss had finally scarred over, only to be wounded yet again. For both Karol and his country, this process occurred over and over.

By the summer of 1941, Hitler broke his pact with Stalin and invaded the Soviet Union. Now Germans occupied all of Poland. Karol continued working and writing poetry, but he underwent an internal transformation. He abandoned his plans to study literature and theater and decided to become a priest. Later he said this process of change was like "being uprooted from the soil in which . . . my humanity had grown."[10] It was the right decision for him. The war, his father's death, and the terrors of the German occupation all combined to create what Karol would later call an "inner fact of . . . absolute clarity . . ."[11] He knew his goal and what sacrifices it required, and he did not look back.

In November 1942, Karol told Father Figelwicz he wanted to become a priest. Figelwicz took him to see Archbishop Adam Sapieha immediately to make secret arrangements. Under German rule, studying to become a priest could result in death.

As German oppression escalated, Karol took refuge in the archbishop's residence and later joined Sapieha's secret seminary. The students

BLACK SUNDAY

On Black Sunday—August 6, 1944—Karol's life was spared. During the summer, Poles in Warsaw had launched a violent rebellion. To prevent a similar uprising in Kraków, German soldiers went house to house, rounding up men and boys for execution or deportation. They tramped through the upper floors of Karol's house. However, they did not enter the basement, where Karol stood quaking behind the door. Afterward, a friend came to check on him. He found Karol lying facedown on the floor, his arms stretched out in the shape of a cross.

were given priests' cassocks and false identity cards in case Gestapo approached them. Karol lived at the archbishop's until the end of war in 1945. The Soviets liberated Kraków on January 19, and the Germans made their final surrender to Allied forces on May 7, 1945. World War II was over, and Poland was free.

But Karol and his Polish countrymen did not realize they had traded one oppressor for another. As Karol prepared to take his vows as a priest, his homeland was sucked into a dark era from which it would not emerge for more than four decades.

The Archbishop Seminary is located near Wawel Castle in Kraków.

CHAPTER
FOUR

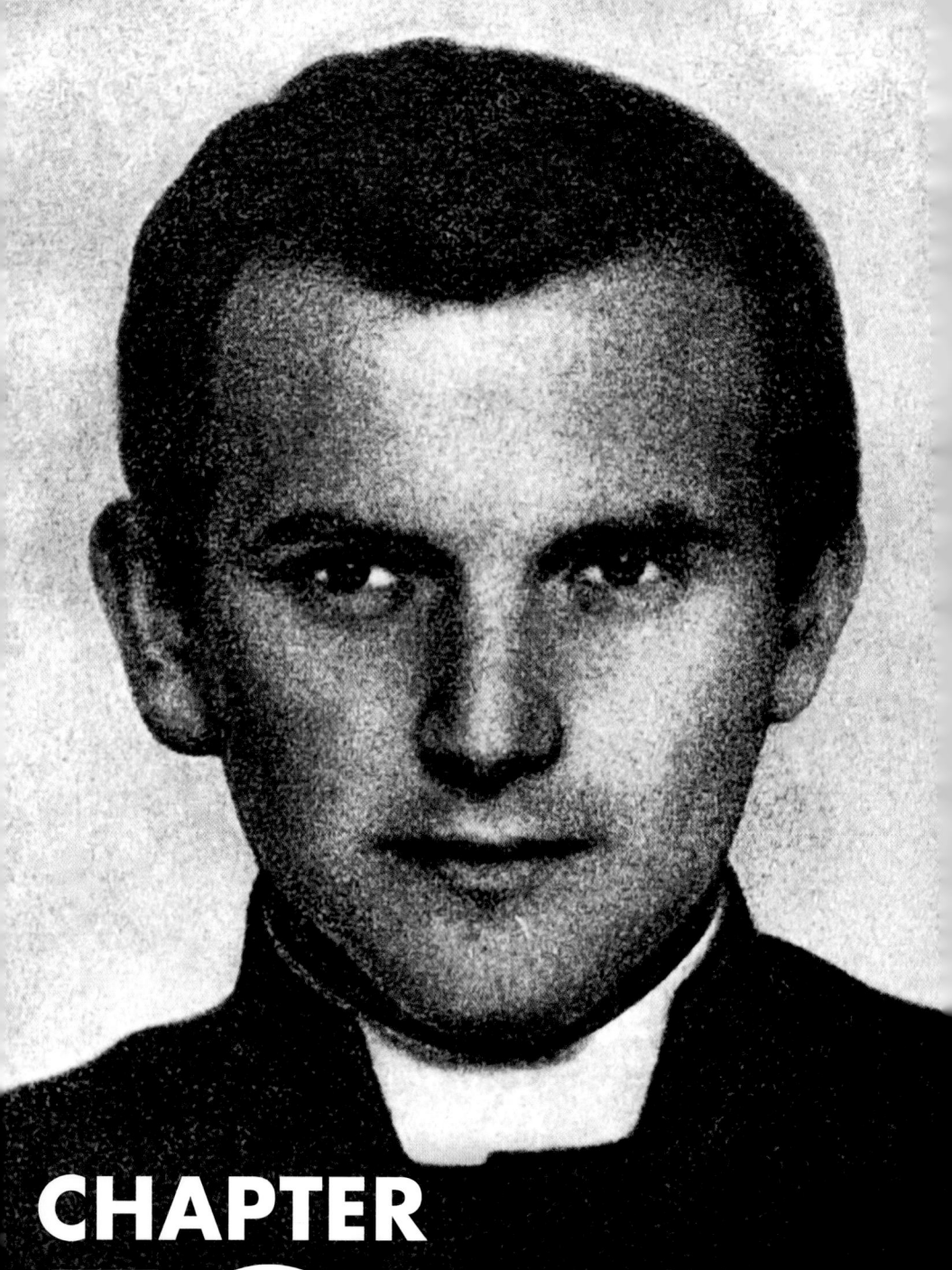

RISE THROUGH THE CHURCH

On November 1, 1946, Catholics throughout Poland flocked to cemeteries carrying candles, flowers, and religious icons in observation of All Saint's Day. Priests performed Mass in an assembly-line fashion throughout the day. It was a sacred day when Poles remembered dead loved ones, but Wojtyla was not at his family's graveside.

Wojtyla was lying prostrate on the marble floor of the archbishop's private chapel, his arms outstretched in the form of a cross. With this act, he willingly submitted himself to God's ministry. Archbishop Sapieha laid his hands upon Wojtyla and performed the sacrament of the Holy Orders. Sacraments are sacred rites or symbols that allow Catholics to see God's power and presence in their lives. No fellow seminary students were lying beside him. Archbishop Sapieha had scheduled Wojtyla's

By being ordained a priest, Wojtyla completely devoted his life to God.

ordination into the priesthood early because he had special plans for this 26-year-old.

Communist Takeover

Even as Poles celebrated the end of World War II, another oppressive force was moving into their country. During the war, Polish Communist leaders had taken refuge in the Soviet Union capital of Moscow, which was

RANKS OF THE CATHOLIC CHURCH

A hierarchy, or ruling body organized into ranks, governs the Catholic Church. The hierarchy is like a pyramid. At the top is the pope, followed by cardinals, archbishops, bishops, priests, and deacons. During the sacrament of Holy Orders, also called ordination, bishops, priests, and deacons are officially given the authority to spread God's message and lead other Catholics. Bishops, priests, and deacons form the base of the Catholic Church hierarchy. Deacons are the lowest ranking and act as assistants to priests and bishops. Priests are responsible for leading religious ceremonies and preaching to a specific congregation.

A diocese is a district containing multiple congregations and is overseen by a bishop. Bishops also ordain new priests and deacons within their diocese. Archbishops oversee other bishops and dioceses in a particular region. Archbishops are not superior in authority to bishops, but their diocese may be more metropolitan. Cardinals act as assistants and advisers to the pope. In particular, cardinals are responsible for electing a pope whenever there is a vacancy. The pope is part of an unbroken line of popes tracing back to Saint Peter, one of Jesus's twelve apostles and the first pope. The pope acts as the supreme leader of the Catholic Church.

the center of the Communist Party. After the defeat of Germany, exiled Communists reentered Poland along with the Soviet Union's Red Army. Under communism, the press was censored and most religion was banned. The government controlled politics, the economy, and education.

Communist leaders feared the Catholic Church. Poland's faith was intense, and religion was linked to national identity. Also, many priests and nuns had worked secretly to resist the Nazis. The Soviet Union feared the church would resist Poland's Communist government as well. This fear was well placed.

Communists rigged the Polish elections held in 1947. As a result, Communist Party members filled all government offices, with Stalin as leader. Something similar was happening in countries across Eastern Europe. This period of Communist oppression would last until 1991 and become known as the Cold War era.

The Peoples' Pastor

In November 1946, Karol registered at the Angelicum, a Catholic university in Rome, Italy, to complete his doctorate. By this time, Poland's Communist government had arrested approximately 700 priests.[1]

> **ACTIVE PRIEST**
>
> Wojtyla loved physical exercise and liked to hike, kayak, and ski. He told a journalist, "I wish I could be out there now, somewhere in the mountains, racing down into a valley; it's an extraordinary sensation."[2] In 1954, Wojtyla won an award from the Polish Tourist Society for the distance he had hiked, getting extra credit for hikes during the winter. Wojtyla maintained his fitness even as he aged. While camping in 1978, 58-year-old Wojtyla swam back and forth across a 900-yard (820 m) lake without stopping.

But Wojtyla was brilliant and had connections. He could have finagled a position in Rome rather than return to Poland. When a friend asked Wojtyla if he was afraid to go home, Wojtyla said yes, but the people needed him. On June 25, 1948, Wojtyla boarded a train headed for Poland to begin his service as a priest.

Wojtyla became assistant pastor at the poor country parish of Niegowici, approximately 30 miles (50 km) east of Kraków. Neither his church nor the little shack where he slept had electricity, running water, or a sewer system. Wojtyla traveled by horse cart to teach at four surrounding village schools.

But Wojtyla had always been unconcerned with material comforts and did not mind this rustic lifestyle. When Wojtyla first arrived in town, he asked a local man for directions. The man later recalled Wojtyla

Wojtyla particularly enjoyed serving young people as a priest.

"wore shabby trousers, a waistcoat, worn-out shoes, and carried a briefcase that I would be ashamed to take with me to market."[3]

Wojtyla enjoyed life as a small town pastor. He instructed children, counseled troubled neighbors, and listened to confessions. But Wojtyla did not sugarcoat the challenges of life when he described it to a friend, saying, "By evening, you feel you can hardly go a step further, but you have to because you know people have been waiting for this visit all year."[4]

In 1949, Archbishop Sapieha called back Wojtyla from his rural post and assigned him to Saint Florian's Church in Kraków. Wojtyla was a chaplain to university students there. The college curriculum was steeped in Communist ideology, so Wojtyla organized off-campus seminars to expose students to other ways of viewing the world. He used drama as a way of teaching them about God.

Although Wojtyla did not teach politics, Communist leaders knew the dangers of encouraging open-minded thinking and worried priests were cooperating with antigovernment groups. The government weakened the Catholic Church by creating Pax, a government-sponsored group of patriotic priests who

Wojtyla organized kayaking and camping trips with groups of his students.

followed the orders of the Communist government rather than the Vatican in Rome. If a priest was not in Pax, he could be arrested on false charges. In just a couple of nights, police arrested more than 11,000 Catholics.[5] The government closed 11 of the 13 Polish seminaries. It closed church schools, took over church-run hospitals, and seized church land. Government spies also infiltrated all levels of the church, from the office of the archdiocese to the monasteries and convents. Some clergy were blackmailed with sex scandals or rumors they had collaborated with the Nazis during World War II.

Wojtyla witnessed the hold communism had on his country. He believed all humans had a natural instinct to seek the truth. Man was free to make choices between

SAINT POPE JOHN PAUL II • 41

PROFESSOR WOJTYLA

For many, Wojtyla was an unforgettable teacher. One student said, "While he was among us, we felt that everything was all right. . . . We felt that we could discuss any problem with him; we could talk about absolutely anything."[6] Wojtyla wore a leather aviator's cap instead of a black hat like most professors. Over his priest's cassock, he wore an old, green coat. During breaks, Wojtyla knelt on the floor of the chapel to pray instead of using a cushioned stool. During his lectures, Wojtyla would pace the aisles, staring intently at students. He removed his glasses and rubbed his forehead as he fired off one question after another.

good and evil. Communism, however, reduced those choices and shamed people. Wojtyla believed where there is no freedom of thought, there is no truth. He would battle this oppression from the pulpit.

In 1951, Wojtyla returned to Jagiellonian University to earn a doctorate in philosophy. In order to brainwash young Poles into accepting communism, only government-sponsored youth groups were permitted. While studying, Wojtyla was a chaplain for college students at Saint Florian's and in hidden ways tried to undermine the Communist government.

Rather than formal groups, Wojtyla organized kayaking and camping trips into the mountains with his students. His students teased him because every so often he would zone out and pray even if he was in the middle of something. The students refused to let Wojtyla lead their bike rides in the hills because they were afraid he would drift off into prayer and run into a tree or off a cliff.

Moving Up the Church Ladder

Wojtyla's prominence within the Catholic Church grew in 1958, when he was made bishop of Kraków and traveled to Rome to attend the Second Vatican Council, the first global church council in 90 years. It was time for Wojtyla to make his mark outside of Poland.

Wojtyla told the bishops at the council the church must triumph over men's souls. He said it was time to engage the world outside of the church and start a conversation with nonbelievers. Starting such a conversation required power, and Wojtyla's influence within the church was growing.

In December 1963, Wojtyla was named archbishop of Kraków and four years later, Wojtyla was appointed cardinal on June 28. Although the Vatican normally has sole authority over appointing high-ranking church officials, the Polish government could veto these decisions. Communist leaders approved Wojtyla's selection because they considered him moderate and easy to work with. But they would soon learn this perception was a mistake.

In public Wojtyla seemed above politics, but in secret he worked to foster Catholicism in Poland, as well as in other Eastern European countries where religion was restricted. As cardinal, Wojtyla coordinated cross-country excursions. On these hikes, Polish priests climbed into the hills and strolled across the border into the neighboring country of Czechoslovakia. They smuggled in religious literature and taught Czechoslovakian seminary students. If these priests had been caught, they would have gone to prison.

Under communism, many works of literature were censored or outright banned. Wojtyla organized annual conferences to discuss theater and poetry, which was illegal. A group of almost 40 people, Christians and non-Christians, would gather to read and discuss theatrical works and poetry. It showed freedom of thought was still alive, even if in secret.

Fighting for Human Rights

Eventually, Wojtyla was forced to make a public stand for human rights. In December 1970, miners in the southwestern Polish region of Silesia refused to come up

As a cardinal, Wojtyla spoke out against human injustice.

from the mine unless they received larger food rations of meat. In other Polish cities, industrial workers went on strike over high food prices, and their wives threw stones through the windows of the Communist Party headquarters. In Gdańsk, a city in northern Poland, port workers in shipyards held protest rallies. The army was sent in to squash these rebellions. In Gdańsk and Gdynia, a city in north-central Poland, troops opened fire in the ports. Dozens of workers were killed and thousands were wounded or arrested.

During a New Year's Eve Mass, Wojtyla publicly condemned the ongoing violence in Poland. Wojtyla expressed unity with the workers and called for justice, but not bloodshed.

When the government began drafting seminary students into the military, Wojtyla protested in a personal letter to Communist leaders. Fearing his influence with the people, the government backed down. Wojtyla's sermons and teachings struck at the heart of communism and made the government nervous.

Secret police documents would reveal three occasions between 1973 and 1974 when the police considered arresting Wojtyla. However, they left him alone because they feared making him a martyr for the people. Instead, police increased surveillance of Wojtyla and targeted people close to him. When security forces beat one of Wojtyla's friends, Wojtyla visited him in the hospital and said, "You were beaten instead of me."[7]

Death Steers a Life

In August 1978, while Wojtyla was enjoying a vacation on the shores of a lake near Rome, he received word that Pope Paul VI had died from a massive heart attack. He flew to Rome to attend the funeral and join the conclave to elect the next pope. Wojtyla's name was whispered among the cardinals, but not as a serious candidate for

Pope Paul VI, *left*, led the Catholic Church for 15 years before his death in 1978.

the papacy. After all, there was a perfectly acceptable Italian candidate, Cardinal Luciani.

Luciani was elected to the papacy, becoming Pope John Paul I. Wojtyla returned to Kraków and celebrated the twentieth anniversary of his dedication as bishop on September 28. That same day, Pope John Paul I unexpectedly died. Wojtyla again traveled to Rome to join the conclave to elect a new pope. This time, it would be a year before Wojtyla came home to Poland—this time as Pope John Paul II.

CHAPTER
FIVE

A POPE FOR THE MODERN AGE

The sky was gray the morning of Pope John Paul II's inauguration on October 22, 1978. But Rome's visitors were overflowing with excitement. Royalty, political leaders, and throngs of the faithful filled Saint Peter's Square.

As John Paul sat in his papal throne, his cardinals came forward and knelt before him to show their obedience. When the aging Cardinal Stefan Wyszýski, a fellow Pole, attempted to kneel before the new pope, John Paul quickly rose from his throne and sank to his own knees. He embraced Wyszýski—a gesture of love and humility. Many historians have said John Paul humanized the papacy unlike any man before him.

For centuries, papal inaugurations were full of the same pomp and ritual as the crowning of kings and queens. Golden tiaras were traditionally placed on the new pope's head and the atmosphere was serious and

Even as supreme leader of the Catholic Church, Pope John Paul II remained humble.

formal. Pope Paul VI first gave up the tiara in 1963 during the Second Vatican Council. Pope John Paul II again refused the crown. During the ceremony, a little boy broke through the barricade holding back the crowd. Officials tried to shoo him away, but John Paul scooped the boy into a hug. Embracing children was more his style than wearing a headdress of gold. Then the pope gave a speech that electrified the world, saying,

A SIMPLE MAN

A solitary cross and a painting of the Virgin Mary decorated the walls of Pope John Paul II's Vatican bedroom. A photo of his parents stood on a table by his bed. His study contained a desk with a red leather top and one lamp. He had maintained this simple lifestyle even before he became pope. John Paul was willing to discard physical comforts if self-denial brought him closer to God. His congregation in Niegowici knew he slept on bare floors, so they bought him a featherbed. But he gave it to a woman who had been robbed. Girls in his youth groups made him a quilt. He graciously accepted it but gave it to a family whose mother had recently died. Although people were sometimes offended by his actions, assuming he did not appreciate their gifts, generosity was part of John Paul's character. He always gave away things he was given, even underwear. His only real possessions were an old green coat and a few books.

When he was archbishop, police held him for a couple hours at a mountain checkpoint. His clothes were so raggedy they figured he must have stolen the archbishop's credentials he had provided them. Shortly after he became cardinal, he stayed with an older priest for a couple nights in a mountain home. The priest assumed he was a new priest and kept sending him on errands. He did the errands willingly, never revealing he was a cardinal.

Pope John Paul II greeted the crowd whenever he held a weekly audience at the Vatican.

> *Do not be afraid! Open wide the doors for Christ. To his saving power open the boundaries of states, economic and political systems. . . . Do not be afraid!*[1]

It was as if John Paul had lit a candle in a room that had been dark for years. His message was steeped in religion and faith, but it was also a political message. People across the world listened.

A New Style

John Paul's work ethic was brutal. He entertained guests at breakfast, lunch, and dinner, scheduling multiple

SAINT POPE JOHN PAUL II • 51

meetings in one afternoon and working 18 hours a day. Italian journalist Marco Politi said John Paul "was the first pope in history where we see his feet."[2] His brown loafers would peek out from under his robes, Politi said. Other popes set themselves apart from their followers, but John Paul stood among them.

John Paul refused to be handled by Vatican officials. He held public audiences every week. After speaking, the pope plunged into the crowd to shake hands with the attendees. When his staff tried to hurry him from one event to another, he said, "I'm the pope. I'll leave when I want to leave."[3]

Traditionally, popes would maintain a regal, formal style when speaking, such as using "we" or "our" when a regular person would say "I" and "my."

REUNITING WITH A FRIEND

During World War II, Karol Wojtyla lost contact with friends from Wadowice, including his best friend Jerzy Kluger. Kluger had suffered during the Holocaust, but survived. When Kluger learned someone named Karol Wojtyla was the archbishop of Kraków, he called to see if it was the same man who had been his best friend in Wadowice. The two men were reunited on October 17, 1978, John Paul's first full day as pope. He received Polish friends in a private ceremony called "Farewell to the Motherland." The name of each person was announced over the loudspeaker to come speak with the new pope. Kluger and his wife were called first.

John Paul tolerated his staff correcting his speech for only a couple of days before telling them to stop. He wanted to speak like a regular person.

When reporters asked the pope if he would continue to ski now that he was pontiff, John Paul replied yes, if they let him. He had been referring to his staff. But this pope did what he wanted. In 1984, dressed in a parka, red boots, and black and white snow pants, the 64-year-old pope skied down a glacier in the Italian Alps. The media loved it. His staff did not.

First Trip Abroad

The jet screeched to a halt on the runway in Santo Domingo, Dominican Republic, on January 25, 1979. John Paul emerged first, followed by a crowd of journalists. Wearing a white gown, the pope looked like a saint. Then he kneeled on the tarmac and kissed the ground, stunning the crowd. John Paul would kiss the ground of every country he visited until his body grew too frail.

At this time, the region was filled with conflict. Civil wars were raging in the Latin American countries of Guatemala, El Salvador, and Nicaragua. The poor allied with Communists against governments supported

> ### SEIZING THE DAY
>
> Every morning, John Paul rose at 5:30 a.m. without an alarm clock. He put on his chasuble, a large poncho-like garment worn by priests. He would conduct a private Mass for approximately 20 guests—politicians, church officials, and ordinary people who had requested the honor. Afterwards, they shared breakfast. The typical menu included eggs, ham, cheese, sausage, and Italian rolls. Breakfast was often John Paul's main meal of the day.

by the rich. These governments terrorized the poor with military forces. The wealthy in Latin America opposed communism, which would redistribute their property among the poor. Since colonial times, the church maintained close ties to the rich. But many priests and bishops joined the new liberation theology movement. This movement believed the church should sever ties with the wealthy and work with the poor despite their connection to Communists.

But John Paul disagreed with this movement. In his first speech in Puebla, Mexico, he scolded the clergy, telling them they were not political leaders. He said priests must be "agent[s] of unity and brotherhood."[4] The Mexican press criticized him for these statements. After all, the pope was giving a speech not far from the border of Guatemala where, in the last few years, tens

Despite political and theological issues in the region, the pope's first trip abroad to Latin America was considered a success.

of thousands of citizens had been murdered by their own government.

John Paul was sensitive to the negative response. He listened to his critics and spoke more gently, saying he wanted to be the voice of those who were silenced and he wanted to defend those who were oppressed.

CHAPTER
SIX

CONFRONTATIONS AND VICTORY

On June 2, 1979, John Paul landed in Warsaw, Poland, and from the moment he kissed the ground, public adoration carried him for nine solid days. The nation was in ecstasy at the return of its native son.

It was a pivotal time in the pope's struggle against communism. At least 10 million of the country's 35 million people saw John Paul II in person.[1] John Paul conducted Mass in Warsaw's Victory Square in front of 500,000 people. John Paul wiped away a tear as he called on the Holy Spirit to "renew the face of the earth—of *this* land!"[2]

The country was a powder keg, and one word from John Paul could have ignited a revolution. But he never mentioned politics and simply acted as though the government did not exist. Rather than confront Communist leaders, the pope hoped to push them toward democracy.

John Paul wears a traditional Polish highlander's gown during his first visit to Poland as pope in 1979.

In the next year, Poland set off on a political rollercoaster that would last throughout the 1980s. The economy was in free fall, the government oppressive and corrupt. On August 14, 1980, workers went on strike at the Gdańsk shipyard. They listed their demands: an independent, self-governing trade union, freedom of speech, freedom of the press, and an end to religious discrimination. The Polish people stood behind the workers, forcing the government to concede to some of their demands. Lech Walesa, the leader of the striking workers, signed the agreement with government representatives. Walesa used a giant pen capped by a portrait of Pope John Paul II. The workers named their union Solidarity.

Poland was not quite ready for democracy, however, and the Communists were still in control. But John Paul had reawakened Polish consciousness and identity.

Gunshots in Saint Peter's Square

On May 13, 1981, Turkish assassin Mehmet Ali Agca waited for the right moment. John Paul gave his usual weekly address and then rode around Vatican Square in a Jeep. As the pope came closer, Agca fired a pistol at the pope. John Paul was shot in the abdomen, and the bullet

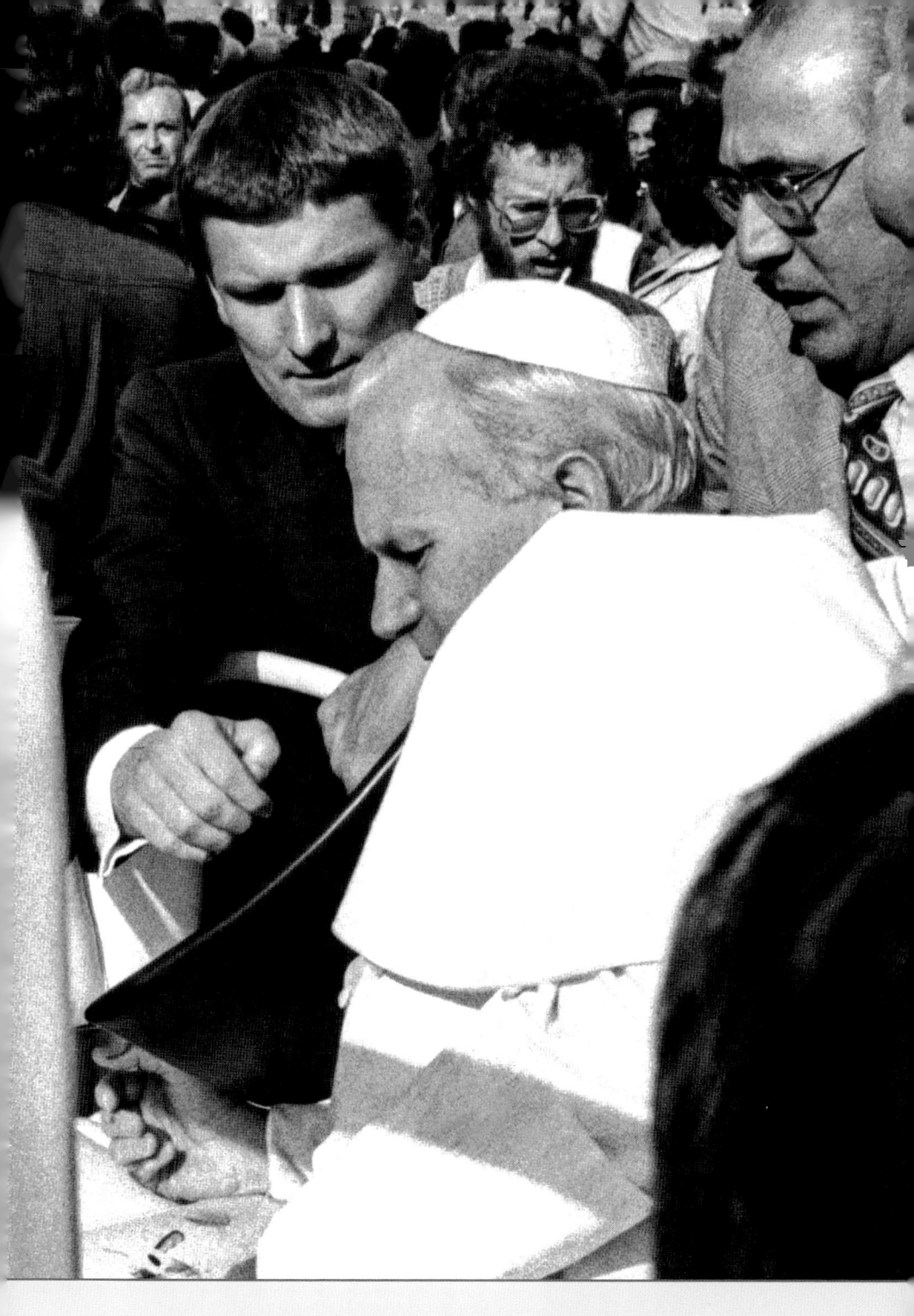

Bodyguards help the pope after an assassination attempt on May 13, 1981.

POPEMOBILE

For centuries, popes rode in carriages or were carried in chairs, allowing the faithful to see them from a distance. But this changed with the invention of the automobile. In 1930, Pope Pius XI received a Mercedes-Benz Nürburg 460 as a present from the company's owner. Since then, Mercedes-Benz and the Vatican have had a solid partnership, although various car manufacturers have produced a version of the Popemobile. After the assassination attempt in 1981, the Popemobile had bulletproof windows on all sides as protection during outdoor appearances. The first was a Range Rover with an enclosed, bulletproof cabin, which the pope rode in during a 1982 visit to the United Kingdom. But open-air Popemobiles still made appearances. When the pope visited Spain in 1982, Spanish car manufacturer SEAT produced an open-air vehicle with handrails so the pope could stand and greet the crowd.

shattered his colon and small intestine. It missed his aorta, an artery that carries blood to the body's organs, by millimeters.

Even after the attempt on his life, the Pope returned to work at the Vatican the first week in June. The assassination attempt, he later said, had been a divine test. He believed God had allowed him to experience suffering in order to understand the grace God also bestowed on him. In 1983, John Paul visited Agca in prison and forgave him.

Martial Law in Poland

In December 1981, the Polish government declared a state of emergency and implemented martial law. A curfew was enforced and soldiers stood on every corner. Communication outside of the country was severed. In December alone, 5,000 Poles were arrested.[3]

John Paul continued to pray for his homeland and repeatedly used the word "solidarity" in his speeches. However, he was also cautious not to agitate the Polish people, which could lead to a civil war. A civil war would give the Soviet Union an excuse to invade.

On Christmas Eve in 1981, a lit candle was placed on the windowsill of the papal apartment overlooking Saint Peter's Square. This was the international symbol of standing with Solidarity. On January 1, 1982, the World Day of Peace, John Paul condemned the "false peace of totalitarian regimes."[4]

Violence in Latin America

In addition to the situation in Poland, Latin America was also becoming a concern the pope needed to address. Violence had increased against members of the Catholic clergy in Latin American countries, particularly El Salvador. The head of the church in the tiny, poor, and violence-ravaged nation was Archbishop Oscar Romero. The murder and abuse of the clergy had radicalized Romero. Starting in 1977, Romero issued powerful sermons from the pulpit against El Salvador's government, which he was sure had supported the murders of the clergy.

Some clergy in Latin America had connections with the rich and with the military controlling the El Salvadoran government. These officials wrote to the Vatican, stating Romero's stance could support a solution such as communism. John Paul had always opposed the liberation theology movement from its beginnings. While he sympathized with the poor in El Salvador, he rejected the ties some Latin American priests had with Communists. After living under communism in Poland, John Paul had seen how this

PAPAL VACATIONS

John Paul took his vacations just as serious as his work as pope. He often spent one to two weeks in silent contemplation. He liked to go to the Dolomite Mountains in Italy because they reminded him of hiking as a youth in Poland.

Once while hiking on a mountain trail, he passed a man sitting in the doorway of his mountain chalet cleaning mushrooms. The man thought this stranger looked familiar. But the stranger was dressed in trousers and a sweater, not the cassock of a clergyman.

The man asked, "Are you the pope? You look just like him!"[5] John Paul answered, "Well that's because I am him. And I apologize for causing such a stir everywhere I go."[6] The man was disappointed because his wife had gone down to the village on an errand, causing her to miss the pope. To console the man, John Paul produced a rosary from his pocket for the man to give to his wife. The man invited John Paul to rest his legs for a while, and the two of them shared a plate of mushrooms and a glass of orangeade.

system stripped people of their freedoms. He believed liberation theology was a way for the Communists to pretend they were in favor of social reforms long enough to take power and install another form of oppression.

Romero met with John Paul at the Vatican in May 1979 and told him about the murders of several priests by government death squads. The pope cautioned Romero to preach about broad principles of human rights, rather than accuse specific people of murder, because he might be wrong.

However, Romero did not back down when he returned to El Salvador. From the pulpit each week Romero listed the latest victims of violence and how they had died. He collected news clippings about John Paul's speeches against recent terrorist acts in Italy. He said if John Paul lived in El Salvador he would also speak out about the violence around him. Romero appealed to the military and National Guard, reminding them they were El Salvadoran and were killing their own people. In response, death squads bombed the church radio station and the library of El Salvador's Catholic university.

John Paul was angry because he had ordered Romero and other bishops to cease their political activism, but they had ignored him. He decided to punish them by reassigning them to another country. Before he could act, however, tragedy struck. On March 24, 1980, Romero said Mass in a hospital chapel and was shot through the chest while raising his hands in prayer. As he lay dying, Romero's last words were for his murderer: "May God have mercy on the assassin."[7] Over time, John Paul's resistance to liberation theology moderated. He saw the poor at the mercy of exploitation by big corporations. In 1988, he returned to Latin America and listened to hungry miners in Bolivia, even wearing a miner's helmet. He spoke about basic human rights, insisting workers needed their daily bread. In a letter to Catholic bishops titled "On Social Concern," the pope wrote neither communism nor capitalism would solve every problem. He said:

> *The all-consuming desire for profit, and the thirst for power, with the intention of imposing one's will upon others . . . are . . . opposed to the will of God . . . and the good of neighbor.*[8]

Confronting a Past of Intolerance

The history of the Catholic Church is peppered with acts of anti-Semitism. Previous popes had issued statements

Archbishop Romero angered El Salvador's government by using his sermons to speak out against injustices.

demonizing Jews and stirring up fears among Christians, which caused them to violently persecute their Jewish neighbors. During the first decade of his papacy, John Paul tried to mend some of these old wounds.

When he first visited Poland as pope in 1979, John Paul prayed at Auschwitz, the most notorious concentration camp. It was where the Nazis had murdered millions of European Jews. John Paul said, "The very people that received from God the commandment 'Thou shalt not kill,' itself experienced in special measure what is meant by killing."[9]

In 1986, in an even stronger act of symbolism, John Paul prayed at the main synagogue in Rome—the first recorded time a pope had ever visited a Jewish holy temple. John Paul also worked to start a dialogue with other faiths. He hosted a World Day of Prayer for Peace on October 27, 1986, and invited 160 religious leaders to gather in Assisi, Italy. These leaders represented faiths from all over the world, including Buddhism, Hinduism, Judaism, Islam, and other Christian religions.

Victory at Last

In 1983, John Paul made a second trip home to Poland, where life was grim. John Paul had postponed a visit

Religious leaders of various faiths gathered in Assisi, Italy, for World Day of Prayer for Peace.

to Poland the previous year because of the unstable situation there. Poles were losing hope, and the Solidarity movement's efforts were waning. To show life in Poland was normal under communism, Poland's new Soviet premier, General Wojciech Jaruzelski, allowed John Paul to meet with leaders of the Solidarity movement.

> **FIGHTING ANTI-SEMITISM**
>
> In 1968, Communists stirred up another anti-Semitic campaign, and 34,000 Jews fled Poland.[10] The Catholic Church did not speak out. But John Paul, who was a cardinal at the time, made a symbolic personal gesture of support for Jews. He visited the synagogue in the Jewish district of Kraków, something no cardinal had ever done. When John Paul later made his 1986 historic visit to the Roman synagogue as pope, he condemned acts of anti-Semitism "at any time and by anyone. I repeat, by anyone."[11] The crowd was made up mostly of Jews, some who had survived the Nazi death camps. The pope's audience gave him a thundering applause.

The pope privately told Solidarity leader Lech Walesa to slow down, saying the church and the union had time. They could agitate for changes, then back off a bit, then agitate some more, and continue this process until they wore down the government. John Paul was in the revolution for the long haul, but insisted on a nonviolent approach.

This strategy was ultimately a success. On June 4, 1989, Poland held the first truly free elections in post-World War II Eastern Europe. In the election, the Solidarity Party won by a landslide. It was the beginning of the end of Communist domination of Eastern Europe.

The Soviet Union's more moderate new leader, Mikhail Gorbachev, started loosening Soviet control from Moscow, which allowed democratic movements to flourish. Gorbachev said he had read John Paul's writing and liked his "concept of the human being, not society, as the center of concern."[12] On November 9, 1989, the Berlin Wall, the physical symbol of the division between Eastern and Western Europe, was torn down in Germany. The Cold War had ended.

Pope John Paul II had many achievements during his first decade as pope. However, the second decade of John Paul's papacy would not allow him to bask in his success. The 1990s would be full of painful divisions. This time the wounds did not come from outside the church—they came from within.

POWERFUL MEETING

The press recorded a meeting between Polish premier General Jaruzelski and John Paul in 1986. Television cameras panned from Jaruzelski's face down to his toes. The man's knees visibly trembled, causing journalists to wonder if he had a medical condition. But ABC News correspondent Bill Blakemore said Jaruzelski later explained, "I was trembling in awe at the responsibility and importance of this man in front of me."[13] Blakemore, who traveled with the pope on 21 international visits, said, "The Pope had this kind of authenticity of nationhood—if you will—of importance. So that even Jaruzelski himself was put on notice that he was in front of the master."[14]

CHAPTER
SEVEN

TROUBLE IN THE SECOND DECADE

During a trip in the early 1990s, John Paul chatted in the back of an airplane with journalists. David Willey of the British Broadcasting Corporation asked a daring question: "Holy Father, you know that there's going to be millions . . . of children born every year in this world . . . who are bound to die young and who will live lives of depravity [evil]. . . . How . . . can you object to artificial birth control?"[1] The pope's reply was quick. He said, "The answer is, as it always was, responsible parenthood."[2]

With the death of communism, the pope believed the church faced an enemy just as dangerous—a modern world in which God, faith, and the rules of the church seemed irrelevant. A Gallup Poll taken in the summer of 1992 revealed many US Catholics did not agree with some core principles of the church. Two out of three Catholics believed women should be able to become

Pope John Paul II traveled to the United States in 1979, 1987, 1993, 1995, and 1999.

71

priests and 75 percent thought priests should be allowed to marry.[3] Battles over these social issues would divide the church throughout the decade.

Birth Control and Abortion Controversies

The United Nations (UN) and the Catholic Church declared 1994 the Year of the Family. The UN organized a conference on population in Cairo, Egypt, which was scheduled for September. In February, John Paul wrote a "Letter to the Family," which addressed the sacredness of the family and the life of the unborn. The letter reinforced the church's position that abortion and contraception were sins.

Meanwhile, human rights groups, health organizations, and the US government had lobbied for the conference to create policies making access to contraception and abortion easier for women.

TRAVELING POPE

John Paul was a pilgrim. He spent 540 days of his papacy on the road, more than any other pope. He visited 129 nations and gave 2,372 speeches, many in countries never previously visited by a pope. All in all, he had traveled 720,284 miles (1,159,185 km) as of October 2003, a distance that would have taken him to the moon and back three times.[4]

They worried about high population growth rates in poor countries. At the time, the global population was an estimated 5.7 billion. The UN wanted to stabilize it at 7.2 billion by 2050.[5] Many health experts also wanted to stop the spread of AIDS, which was killing millions of people, particularly on the continent of Africa. A key document authored mainly by the International Planned Parenthood Federation called for massive contraception distribution and referred to "reproductive health" and "reproductive rights."[6]

John Paul believed these initiatives threatened the sacredness of life and were an attempt to make

CALLS FOR PEACE

John Paul's opposition to abortion and contraception was part of his broader fight for the dignity of human life. Throughout his papacy, he used every opportunity to tell the world to reduce violence. John Paul was also against war between nations. John Paul was a consistent, passionate spokesman for peace. In August 1990, the Middle Eastern country of Iraq invaded its neighbor, Kuwait. While the United States led a coalition of western and Middle Eastern countries to prepare for war, John Paul called for peace.

On Christmas Day in 1990, the pope gave a message to the world. He said:

The light of Christ is with the tormented Nations of the Middle East. For the area of the Gulf, we await with trepidation for the threat of conflict to disappear. May leaders be convinced that war is an adventure with no return![7]

Even as the First Gulf War erupted in January 1991, John Paul made 25 more appeals for peace.

abortion a protected right under international law. As the conference drew near, John Paul fought back. He wrote a personal letter to the heads of all the governments in the world and to the secretary general of the United Nations. He urged them to reject the proposal by Planned Parenthood, saying it "could cause a moral decline resulting in a serious setback for humanity."[8]

The Vatican was not blind to the problems of overpopulation in underdeveloped countries. But the pope believed poverty, health care, and education for the poor needed to be solved through economic policies, not birth control. He wanted the UN to increase its funding for population control, but he called for this money to be used toward economic initiatives. John Paul was concerned about the huge gap between rich nations and underdeveloped countries,

---

CULTURE OF DEATH

The modern world troubled John Paul. In 1995, he wrote a letter addressed to all Catholics titled "The Gospel of Life." In it, he reinforced the Catholic Church's position on valuing human life. In this letter, John Paul said, "Whatever is opposed to life itself, such as any type of murder, genocide, abortion, euthanasia . . . whatever insults human dignity, such as subhuman living conditions . . . disgraceful working conditions . . . all these things . . . poison human society . . . are a supreme dishonor to the Creator."[9] John Paul feared the growing influence of what he characterized as a culture of death.

primarily in Africa, Asia, and Latin American. He criticized the damage caused by "savage capitalism."[10]

In the spring of 1994, a commission met to discuss the population agreement and decided to adopt the "reproduction health" concepts from the original Planned Parenthood document. John Paul was so alarmed he contacted US President Bill Clinton, the primary supporter of the new policies. The two men met at the Vatican on June 2.

Clinton and John Paul had a civil conversation but reached no agreement, with Clinton later saying they had a fundamental difference of opinion. Clinton was pro-choice, meaning he supported the choice to have an abortion, and his administration supported family planning efforts including contraception. John Paul, however, was steadfastly opposed to the document having any language stating abortion would ever be permitted.

Bishops across the globe took the pope's campaign worldwide, urging their governments to resist any international agreements making abortion and birth control more accessible to women in underdeveloped countries. The Clinton administration ultimately backed down, and the final UN agreement was a victory

The pope and President Clinton differed greatly on birth control and abortion policies.

for John Paul—in a way. It did not expand abortion or contraception programs. Even the distribution of condoms as a way to prevent AIDS was removed from the final document. John Paul believed he was defending life and the family. However, people around the world criticized him for opposing some of these programs, which could save lives and ease burdens on women in poor countries.

The Church and Women

Some tensions between US Catholics and John Paul had ignited during his first trip to the United States in

1979 and continued into the second decade of his papacy. One issue was the church's ban on contraception, as well as prohibiting women from being ordained as priests.

Because the apostles, the original followers of Jesus, were men, the Catholic Church has traditionally not allowed women to become priests. However, many Catholics, especially in the United States and Europe, began to reject this position as outdated and sexist. But John Paul refused to bend.

> **VIEW ON HOMOSEXUALITY**
>
> In 1987, John Paul visited an AIDS clinic for homosexuals in San Francisco, California. One of the dying patients he consoled was a priest. The pope told the men God loved them without limits. However, these words did not satisfy Catholic homosexuals. He had repeatedly called homosexuality a "moral evil" and insisted homosexuals should remain celibate.[11] Also, he forbade priests from mentioning condoms as disease prevention devices when they counseled homosexuals.

In 1994, he sent a letter to world bishops stating the church had no authority whatsoever to ordain women as priests. He referred to the example of the Virgin Mary. She was the mother of Jesus Christ and had never been one of Jesus' chosen followers or called on to be a minister. To John Paul it was evidence, not of women's inferiority, but how different roles for men and women were part of God's plan.

Women are allowed to serve only as nuns or nonordained members in the church hierarchy.

This statement fueled discussion among Catholics everywhere, but in the last part of his letter John Paul banned any further debate on the subject. It was the first time in modern history the church had prohibited free discussion on a topic. Many women were indignant, but John Paul did not budge.

The pope did not intend to alienate or oppress women. So a month later, he gave a message to all priests stating the church recognizes the value of women as part of the Christian "awareness of the value of every person."[12] This statement did not satisfy women in western nations. The ordination of women as priests has continued to be a controversial topic in the church into the 2010s.

Evangelization or Cultural Imperialism

The number of Catholics in the world grew during the 1900s, particularly in Africa. In 1900, there were only 2 million Catholics in Africa. In 2000, there were almost 100 million.[13] However, some clergy argued the church's mission of evangelizing, or spreading the word of the Bible, was over. They worried teaching Catholic beliefs to non-Christians was a form of cultural imperialism, or extending domination over another country. John Paul decided as the third millennium of Christianity approached in the year 2000, he needed to say something about the future of the church as an evangelizer.

On December 7, 1990, the pope wrote "the Mission of the Redeemer." In this letter, John Paul said one's faith is strengthened when it is spread to others, and Christianity was full of good news about God that needed to be shared. John Paul said everyone, everywhere should be evangelized to, including

John Paul II's visits to Africa are said to have contributed to Catholicism's growth on the continent.

non-Christians and those within the church who have fallen away from their faith. The pope was the ideal example of such evangelism. In 1990 alone, he toured five African countries, calling people to the faith.

But there was also difficulty in finding people to minister to the faithful. John Paul could not seem to understand why there was a decline in the number of men and women willing to dedicate their lives to the church. Between 1979 and 1990, the number of priests declined by 4 percent. The problem was particularly strong in the United States, where for every ten retiring priests there were only six to replace them. Some bishops suggested perhaps the church should relax the restrictions on celibacy, or the rule prohibiting priests from marrying or having sexual relations. Recruiting older men, even if they were married, would shore up the numbers of priests in the world. John Paul dismissed this suggestion. He believed living a celibate life showed the world a man was committed to God. The pope believed society needed the example of such faith in the troubled modern world.

CHAPTER EIGHT

THE FINAL YEARS

Two million young people made the pilgrimage to Rome in the summer of 2000. The Italian press called them "Pope-hooligans" and "Papa boys."[1] Temperatures were high and crowds were doused with hoses to keep cool. The youth visited holy sites, attended lectures, and gave theatrical performances. They also celebrated Mass with Pope John Paul II in Saint Peter's Square. The crowd was so large the pope looked like a piece of "white confetti" up on the balcony.[2] These World Youth Days formed the heart of the Golden Jubilee celebration.

In the Old Testament, a jubilee is a time to take stock of one's life and make changes. The Golden Jubilee of 2000 would prepare believers to lead Christian lives in the third millennium.

John Paul II modeled a fresh start by formally apologizing for the past sins of the church. The list was long: the Crusades, the Inquisition, and the Holocaust. The pope also reached out to other religions. While his

People traveled from all over the world to celebrate the Golden Jubilee.

> **VISIT TO A MUSLIM MOSQUE**
>
> In May 2001, John Paul entered the Umayyad Mosque in Syria, becoming the first pope in history to visit a Muslim mosque. This visit was part of his efforts to heal the deep divisions among the three religions worshiping the same god. Sheik Ahmad Kuftaro welcomed him. There is long-standing hostility between Islamic nations and the Jewish state of Israel, but John Paul said, "In this holy land Christians, Muslims and Jews are called to work together," for "the day when the legitimate rights of all people are respected."[6]

overtures to Greek Orthodox Christians and Muslims were only moderately successful, the pope went a long way toward mending relations with Jews. However, as the Jubilee year ended, a dark period for the church began.

Clerical Abuse Scandal

On January 6, 2002, a headline in the *Boston Globe* newspaper horrified the world: "Church Allowed Abuse by Priest for Years."[3] For almost 30 years, Priest John Geoghan had inappropriately touched at least 130 children.[4] Church officials in the Archdiocese of Boston had been made aware of the abuse. But they relocated Geoghan three times after therapists reassured them it was "appropriate and safe."[5] At the new parishes, Geoghan continued his predatory behavior.

The church sex abuse scandal took a toll on an aging Pope John Paul II.

Once this story broke, the media discovered Geoghan's case was just the tip of the iceberg. Accusations against other clergy poured in from across the country. A group of US bishops asked the pope for the power to remove priests who had been accused of sexual misconduct with children. But John Paul refused. He cited the years of Communist rule in Poland, when police used false allegations of sexual scandal to destroy the reputations of activist priests.

The scandal grew. Lawyers unearthed mountains of documents that revealed church officials had concealed abuse by priests for decades. For weeks the pope did not make an official statement. Then in a letter issued days before Easter in 2002, John Paul briefly mentioned "the sins of some of our brothers."[7] A Vatican official dismissed reporters' questions, saying the pope had more serious matters to think about. But a media storm followed these remarks and John Paul finally acted.

He called American bishops to Rome for an emergency meeting to clarify his views. He said, "There is no place in the priesthood or religious life for those who would harm the young. . . . To the victims and their families . . . I express my profound sense of solidarity and concern."[8] But some people wondered whether these words were too little and too late.

People questioned John Paul's slow response to the abuse scandal. The Vatican is an ancient institution and not used to the 24-hour news cycle of the digital age. John Paul reacted to events rather than being out in front of them. Also, his experience living under communism made him distrust the media. He believed the press had blown events out of proportion. Most important, the pope spent his life holding the church together in difficult circumstances. He wanted to shield the faithful from anything that might make them doubt their faith.

Farewell to a Pope

Pope John Paul II had experienced a lot of hardship in his life. He had suffered under the Nazi and Soviet occupations in Poland. He had been hit by a truck and left for dead. He had survived an assassin's bullet in 1981. He also endured a stomach tumor in 1992, a broken shoulder in 1993, a hip replacement in 1994, and was diagnosed with Parkinson's disease in 1991. Parkinson's disease made walking a challenge for John Paul. His limbs trembled and his face took on a frozen expression, his head at an awkward tilt. Even as some people wondered if he should retire, John Paul kept on, saying, "you cannot come down from the cross."[9]

By the fall of 2003, it was obvious the pope was in pain. At an event in Slovakia, he was unable to finish his

> **PARKINSON'S DISEASE**
>
> Parkinson's disease affects approximately one percent of the population over 65. The disease causes a shortage of dopamine, the hormone that regulates the motor skills of the limbs. Parkinson's dopamine deficiency causes shaking and stiffness. Some Parkinson's sufferers also have reported mildly weakened cognitive functions, such as difficulties with attention and memory.

remarks. He conducted the ceremony, ordaining 31 new cardinals, but exhaustion carved grooves in his face. People wondered if the pope's death was approaching.

Still John Paul continued serving and even became the third-longest serving pope on March 14, 2004. But the pope froze at the window of his balcony during his final Easter service in 2005. Then he whispered, "My voice is gone."[10] He made the sign of the cross three times, waved to the crowd, and withdrew.

On March 31, 2005, John Paul was preparing Mass in his private chapel. Suddenly, his body jolted as if electrified. He was in septic shock from a urinary tract infection. His staff put him to bed, and a cardinal said Mass at his bedside. His caretakers kissed his hand and prayed. Over the next few days, the pope weakened. Sister Tobiana Sobodka was present and heard his last words when Pope John Paul II whispered, "Let me go to the Father's house."[11]

At 7:00 p.m. on April 2, 2005, the pope slipped into a coma. A crowd stood vigil in Saint Peter's Square. Shortly before 10:00 p.m., Cardinal Leonardo Sandri stepped out onto the balcony and said, "Our beloved Holy Father has gone home to the Father's house."[12]

Thousands gathered at the Vatican as Pope John Paul's casket was carried to Saint Peter's Basilica.

Faithful in John Paul's native Poland commemorated the pope with an outdoor Mass.

Pilgrims flooded into Saint Peter's Square to attend Pope John Paul II's funeral on April 8, 2005. Nuns prayed the rosary, clutching beads in their hands. A long line of priests fanned out into the crowd to give communion to the faithful. Inside the basilica, John Paul lay in a purple-lined wooden coffin. A veil was placed over his face and the coffin was sealed. The vicar of Rome, Cardinal Camillo Ruini, prayed before the coffin.

Twelve pallbearers carried the coffin outside and set it before the altar in front of Saint Peter's. Cardinal Josef Ratzinger of Germany, who would later be named the next pope, gave the sermon and sprinkled holy water on the coffin. After the Mass, the pallbearers hoisted the coffin back onto their shoulders and faced the crowd. They stood for a long moment as the throng applauded Pope John Paul II one last time before he was taken back into the church for burial. The coffin was placed in the grotto beneath Saint Peter's, bells ringing as the pope was laid to rest.

Legacy

In 1978 the world shifted. Popular movements for freedom and justice trembled under the oppressive hand of totalitarian regimes. Into that mix stepped a man with a vision—John Paul. At times he seemed larger than life, jetting around the world and speaking multiple languages in front of millions. After his death, some started calling him John Paul the Great.

John Paul was a pastor to the world. Traditionally, popes had ruled from Rome, safe inside the Vatican's walls. This was not the case for John Paul. He achieved a status similar to a rock star. In 1993, at World Youth

> **SPREADING THE FAITH**
>
> While the number of Catholics in the United States has declined, membership has increased in Africa and Asia. Over the past 30 years, the Catholic population in Africa has tripled to more than 150 million as of 2010. The continent accounts for more than 10 percent of Catholics worldwide. In Asia, the church has more than 100 million followers. The number of Asian and African priests has also increased. Africa and Asia now help supply the rest of the world with priests, with approximately 300 priests from these countries coming to serve parishes in the United States each year.[15]

Day in Denver, Colorado, 90,000 youth packed Mile High Stadium chanting, "John Paul Two, we love you!"[13] In his pilgrimages to more than 100 countries, the pope brought the church to the people and expanded Catholicism in Africa and Asia, continents where the church had been historically absent.

John Paul inspired hope for millions of people trapped behind communism's oppression. His quiet courage spoke truth to those in power and launched a nonviolent revolution. The change in Poland sparked similar movements throughout other Communist countries in Eastern Europe. Journalist Neil Ascherson said what happened in Poland "became the lancehead, which . . . went straight into the bowels of the whole Communist Soviet Empire . . . and . . . it simply didn't recover."[14]

John Paul used his stage as pope to speak out for human rights around the world, giving comfort to people suffocating under poverty and oppression. He declared all life to be sacred, from an unborn child, to an enemy on the battlefield, to his own assassin. Furthermore, John Paul apologized for the church's record of human rights violations.

At times John Paul seemed to be full of many contradictions. While he spoke with moral authority against the Communist regime in Poland, he failed to see how Latin Americans suffered under governments just as oppressive. John Paul revered the Virgin Mary, but closed the door to significant involvement of women in the hierarchy of the church. He preached about the sacredness of all life, but as the global population soared and AIDS killed millions, John Paul opposed programs making contraception more accessible.

However one views John Paul, one fact is indisputable. John Paul charted his own path and changed the world. His mission was to give people the life preserver of faith as they navigated the dangerous tides of the modern world. It is too soon to tell if John Paul achieved this goal. The Catholic Church in the United States and Western Europe is still reeling from

A portrait of Pope John Paul II was on display in Saint Peter's Square during his canonization.

the clerical sex abuse scandal. However, Catholicism has taken root and is growing in Africa and Asia.

On May 1, 2011, Pope Benedict XVI beatified John Paul II. Some questioned the decision because of the sexual abuse scandal during John Paul's papacy. But to many others it was the next step toward sainthood for John Paul II.

Pope Francis officially canonized John Paul II as a saint on April 17, 2014, in front of 500,000 visitors in Saint Peter's Square. John XXIII, pope from

1958 to 1963, was also canonized, making the event unprecedented. For the first time in church history, two former popes were canonized on the same day.

Saint Pope John Paul II was the third-longest serving pope of all time and the longest serving pope of the 1900s. Beloved by his flock, he was seen as a simple man dressed in white, his back slightly hunched and an expression of stern contemplation on his face. For millions, John Paul II was a figure on the mountaintop—ready to light the world with the torch of his faith.

ROAD TO SAINTHOOD

John Paul II's 2011 beatification was the first step on the path toward becoming a saint. The rules on what it takes to be declared a saint have changed over time. Centuries ago, a local church could simply declare someone a saint, which grew messy. In the 1100s, Swedish church leaders declared a priest a saint after he was killed in a drunken brawl. Since then it has become much tougher. The first step is beatification, meaning the person has entered heaven and can intervene to help those who pray to him or her.

Beatification requires the person to be responsible for at least one miracle. The second step is canonization, which means the person has entered the canon, or special group, of saints. This requires a second, verified, miracle. The Vatican credited John Paul with two miracles. The church appoints a Miracle Commission made up of theologians and scientific experts. The first was a French nun cured of Parkinson's disease after praying to him. The second was a Costa Rican woman cured of a brain aneurysm after seeing him on a magazine cover.

TIMELINE

1920
Karol Jozef Wojtyla is born May 18 in Wadowice, Poland.

1929
Karol's mother dies on April 13 of inflammation of the heart and kidneys.

1932
Karol's brother, Edmund, dies from scarlet fever in December.

1939
In August, Karol begins college at the Jagiellonian University in Kraków, Poland; Germany invades Poland on September 1, beginning World War II.

1941
Karol's father dies from a heart attack on February 18.

1946
Wojtyla is ordained as a priest on November 1.

1958
On July 4, Wojtyla is chosen as bishop of Kraków.

1963
Wojtyla is named archbishop of Kraków in December.

1967
Wojtyla is promoted to cardinal on June 28.

1978
The College of Cardinals elects Wojtyla as pope on October 16. He becomes Pope John Paul II.

TIMELINE

1979
From January 25 to February 1, John Paul makes his first trip abroad to the Caribbean and Latin America; John Paul returns to Poland for the first time as pope on June 2.

1981
John Paul is shot in Saint Peter's Square on May 13.

1994
John Paul campaigns against changes to international agreements on abortion and birth control to underdeveloped countries.

2000
John Paul leads the celebration of the Golden Jubilee.

2002
US bishops meet in Rome to discuss the sexual abuse crisis with John Paul in late April.

2004
John Paul becomes the third longest-serving pope in history on March 14.

2005
John Paul suffers septic shock from a urinary tract infection on March 31; he dies on April 2; on April 8, he is laid to rest in the grotto beneath the Vatican.

2011
John Paul is beatified by the Catholic Church on May 1.

2014
Pope Francis canonizes Pope John Paul II as a saint on April 17.

ESSENTIAL FACTS

Date of Birth
May 18, 1920

Place of Birth
Wadowice, Poland

Date of Death
April 2, 2005

Parents
Karol Wojtyla Sr. and Emilia Kaczorowska

Education
Jagiellonian University, Kraków seminary

Career Highlights
John Paul was a priest, archbishop, and a cardinal prior to being elected pope in 1978. He was the third longest-serving pope in history.

Societal Contribution
As archbishop and cardinal, he led the church in Poland during the Cold War when the Communists oppressed religious freedom. Pope John Paul II was the first non-Italian pope in more than 400 years and the first Polish pope in the history of the Catholic Church. During his papacy, he traveled to more countries than any pope in history and spoke out for human rights and against oppression.

He attempted to repair relations with other religions and apologized for the previous intolerance of the church.

Conflicts

Pope John Paul II refused to compromise on the church's position against abortion, contraception, and the ordination of women as priests. This alienated many Catholics in western nations. In 2002, a scandal became public within the church, charging several priests with child sexual abuse. Evidence also revealed church officials had knowledge of these abuses and covered them up. John Paul II was criticized for not doing enough to prevent the abuse within the church.

Quote

"Do not be afraid. Open wide the doors for Christ. To his saving power open the boundaries of states, economic and political systems, the vast fields of culture, civilization and development."—*Pope John Paul II*

GLOSSARY

anti-Semitism
Hatred and discrimination against Jews as a racial or ethnic group.

basilica
A large and important church that is granted special ceremonial privileges by the pope.

beatification
The act of declaring someone as blessed and worthy of being revered by Catholics.

canonization
The act of declaring someone an officially recognized saint.

capitalism
An economic system in which factories, services, and goods are privately owned.

clergy
People ordained to serve God, as well as provide spiritual guidance and perform sacred rituals within the Catholic Church.

Communism
An economic system based on the elimination of private ownership of factories, land, and other means of economic production.

conclave
A private meeting of Catholic cardinals to elect a new pope.

contraception
The use of any method or device to prevent pregnancy.

Holocaust
The mass murder of millions of Jews and other minorities by the Nazis during World War II.

martial law
The temporary rule by military authorities during times of public unrest or war.

martyr
A person who is willing to die or suffer for his or her beliefs.

ordination
The act or ceremony of giving someone the authority to perform the spiritual and religious functions of a church.

seminary
A school or college for training students to be priests, ministers, or rabbis.

Vatican
The official papal residence in Rome, which also serves as the administrative offices of the Catholic Church.

vicar
A representative or deputy of a bishop.

ADDITIONAL RESOURCES

Selected Bibliography

Pigozzi, Caroline. *Pope John Paul II, An Intimate Life: The Pope I Knew So Well*. New York: Faithwords, 2005. Print.

Weigel, George. *The End and the Beginning: Pope John Paul II—The Victory of Freedom, the Last Years, the Legacy*. New York: Doubleday, 2010. Print.

Wojtyla, Karol. *Pope John Paul II: Gift and Mystery. On the Fiftieth Anniversary of my Priestly Ordination*. New York: Doubleday, 1996. Print.

Further Readings

Mainardi, Alessandro. *The Life of Pope John Paul II in Comics*. New York: Papercutz, 2005. Print.

Stanley, George E. *Pope John Paul II: Young Man of the Church*. New York: Aladdin, 2005. Print.

Websites

To learn more about Essential Lives, visit **booklinks.abdopublishing.com**. These links are routinely monitored and updated to provide the most current information available.

Places to Visit

Bishop's Palace and Archdiocese Museum
21 Kanonicza Street
Kraków, Poland
+48-012-421-89-63
http://www.muzeumkra.diecezja.pl/index_en.htm
Pope John Paul II lived here twice: first as a priest and later as archbishop of Kraków, until he became pope in 1978.

The Blessed John Paul II Shrine
3900 Harewood Road Northeast
Washington, DC, 20017
http://www.jp2shrine.org/jp/en/about/index.html
This memorial is dedicated to Pope John Paul II. The shrine includes exhibits on his life and legacy, as well as the role of Catholicism in the United States.

Vatican Museum
Viale Vaticano, 00165
Rome, Italy
+39-06-6988-3332
http://mv.vatican.va/index.html
This is the headquarters of the Roman Catholic Church and official papal residence. The historical site includes Saint Peter's Basilica, the burial site of Saint Peter, the first pope, and many other popes, including John Paul II.

SOURCE NOTES

Chapter 1. A Smoky Sky
1. Jonathan Kwitny. *Man of the Century: The Life and Times of Pope John Paul II*. New York: Holt, 1997. Print. 284.
2. Bob Parker. "Announcement of John Paul II Becoming Pope October 1978." *YouTube*. YouTube, 18 Apr. 2009. Web. 12 May 2015.
3. Ibid.
4. George Weigel. *The End and the Beginning: Pope John Paul II—The Victory of Freedom, the Last Years, the Legacy*. New York: Doubleday, 2010. Print. 95.

Chapter 2. Son of Poland
1. Tad Szulc. *Pope John Paul II: The Biography*. New York: Scribner, 1995. Print. 57.
2. Jonathan Kwitny. *Man of the Century: The Life and Times of Pope John Paul II*. New York: Holt, 1997. Print. 35.
3. Jane Barnes and Helen Whitney. "John Paul II: His Life and His Papacy." *Frontline*. PBS, n.d. Web. 12 May 2015.
4. Tad Szulc. *Pope John Paul II: The Biography*. New York: Scribner, 1995. Print. 77.
5. Karol Wojtyla. *Pope John Paul II: Gift and Mystery. On the Fiftieth Anniversary of My Priestly Ordination*. New York: Doubleday, 1996. Print. 20.
6. Jane Barnes, and Helen Whitney. "John Paul II: His Life and His Papacy." *Frontline*. PBS, n.d. Web. 12 May 2015.
7. Tad Szulc. *Pope John Paul II: The Biography*. New York: Scribner, 1995. Print. 58.
8. Gian Franco Svidercoschi. *Letter to a Jewish Friend: The Simple and Extraordinary Story of Pope John Paul II and His Jewish School Friend*. New York: Crossroad, 1994. Print. 17.
9. Jonathan Kwitny. *Man of the Century: The Life and Times of Pope John Paul II*. New York: Henry Holt and Co., 1997. Print. 39.

Chapter 3. Faith Forged By War
1. Tad Szulc. *Pope John Paul II: The Biography*. New York: Scribner, 1995. Print. 88–93.
2. Jonathan Kwitny. *Man of the Century: The Life and Times of Pope John Paul II*. New York: Holt, 1997. Print. 54–55.
3. Tad Szulc. *Pope John Paul II: The Biography*. New York: Scribner, 1995. Print. 103.
4. Ibid. 109.
5. Karol Wojtyla. *Pope John Paul II: Gift and Mystery. On the Fiftieth Anniversary of My Priestly Ordination*. New York: Doubleday, 1996. Print. 23.

6. "Introduction to the Holocaust." *United States Holocaust Memorial Museum*. United States Holocaust Memorial Council, 20 June 2014. Web. 12 May 2015.

7. "Holocaust Timeline: The Camps." *Holocaust Timeline: The Camps*. Florida Center for Instructional Technology, n.d. Web. 12 May 2015.

8. Dan Ashley. "Museum of the History of Polish Jews Opens in Poland with Help from Bay Area Man." *ABC7 San Francisco*. ABC, 28 Oct. 2014. Web. 12 May 2015.

9. Karol Wojtyla. *Pope John Paul II: Gift and Mystery. On the Fiftieth Anniversary of My Priestly Ordination*. New York: Doubleday, 1996. Print. 21–22.

10. Ibid. 34.

11. Jonathan Kwitny. *Man of the Century: The Life and Times of Pope John Paul II*. New York: Holt, 1997. Print. 76.

Chapter 4. Rise Through the Church

1. Jonathan Kwitny. *Man of the Century: The Life and Times of Pope John Paul II*. New York: Holt, 1997. Print. 105.

2. Ibid. 212.

3. Ibid. 109.

4. Ibid. 113.

5. Ibid. 116.

6. George Weigel. *The End and the Beginning: Pope John Paul II—The Victory of Freedom, the Last Years, the Legacy*. New York: Doubleday, 2010. Print. 41.

7. Ibid. 88.

Chapter 5. A Pope for the Modern Age

1. Jonathan Kwitny. *Man of the Century: The Life and Times of Pope John Paul II*. New York: Holt, 1997. Print. 19.

2. "John Paul II: The Millennial Pope." *Frontline*. Writ. Jane Barnes and Helen Whitney. PBS, 1999. DVD.

3. Jonathan Kwitny. *Man of the Century: The Life and Times of Pope John Paul II*. New York: Holt, 1997. Print. 17.

4. Ibid. 313.

Chapter 6. Confrontations and Victory

1. Tad Szulc. *Pope John Paul II: The Biography*. New York: Scribner, 1995. Print. 303.

SOURCE NOTES CONTINUED

2. George Weigel. *The End and the Beginning: Pope John Paul II—The Victory of Freedom, the Last Years, the Legacy*. New York: Doubleday, 2010. Print. 111.

3. Ibid. 136–137.

4. Ibid. 143.

5. Caroline Pigozzi. *Pope John Paul II, An Intimate Life: The Pope I Knew So Well*. New York: Faithwords, 2005. Print. 172.

6. Ibid.

7. Jonathan Kwitny. *Man of the Century: The Life and Times of Pope John Paul II*. New York: Holt, 1997. Print. 353.

8. Ibid. 576.

9. Ibid. 327.

10. Jane Barnes and Helen Whitney. "John Paul II: His Life and His Papacy." *Frontline*. PBS, n.d. Web. 12 May 2015.

11. E. J. Dionne. "Pope Speaks in Rome Synagogue, in the First Such Visit on Record." *New York Times*. New York Times, 14 Apr. 1986. Web. 12 May 2015.

12. Jonathan Kwitny. *Man of the Century: The Life and Times of Pope John Paul II*. New York: Holt, 1997. Print. 588.

13. "Interview Bill Blakemore." *Frontline*. PBS, n.d. Web. 12 May 2015.

14. Ibid.

Chapter 7. Trouble in the Second Decade

1. Bill Blakemore. "John Paul: The Millennial Pope." *Frontline*. PBS, n.d. Web. 12 May 2015

2. Ibid.

3. Larry Stammer. "Women's Role in Church Divides Catholic Bishops." *Baltimore Sun*. Baltimore Sun Media Group, 19 June 1992. Web. 12 May 2015.

4. Caroline Pigozzi. *Pope John Paul II, An Intimate Life: The Pope I Knew So Well*. New York: Faithwords, 2005. Print. 108.

5. Tad Szul. *Pope John Paul II: The Biography*. New York: Scribner, 1995. Print. 428.

6. Ibid. 427.

7. George Weigel. *Witness to Hope: The Biography of Pope John Paul II*. Harper, 2001. Print. 620.

8. Tad Szul. *Pope John Paul II: The Biography*. New York: Scribner, 1995. Print. 427.

9. Pope John Paul II. "Evangelium Vitae (The Gospel of Life)." *Eternal Word Television Network*. Eternal Word Television Network, n.d. Web. 12 May 2015.

10. Tad Szul. *Pope John Paul II: The Biography*. New York: Scribner, 1995. Print. 428.

11. Jonathan Kwitny. *Man of the Century: The Life and Times of Pope John Paul II*. New York: Holt, 1997. Print. 570.

12. Tad Szul. *Pope John Paul II: The Biography*. New York: Scribner, 1995. Print. 436.

13. George Weigel. *Witness to Hope: The Biography of Pope John Paul II*. Harper, 2001. Print. 633.

Chapter 8. The Final Years

1. Bianchi Gioby. "World Youth Day 2000: A Personal Account." *Independent Catholic News*. Independent Catholic News, 29 Aug. 2000. Web. 12 May 2015.

2. Ibid.

3. Matt Carroll, Sacha Pfeiffer, and Michael Rezendes. "Church Allowed Abuse by Priest for Years." *Boston.com*. New York Times, 6 Jan. 2002. Web. 12 May 2015.

4. Ibid.

5. Ibid.

6. Alessandra Stanley. "Pope, in Damascus, Goes to a Mosque for Unity." *New York Times*. New York Times, 7 May 2001. Web. 12 May 2015.

7. George Weigel. *The End and the Beginning: Pope John Paul II—The Victory of Freedom, the Last Years, the Legacy*. New York: Doubleday, 2010. Print. 289.

8. Ibid. 291.

9. Phillip Puella. "Pope's Sudden Resignation Sends Shockwaves Through Church." *Reuters*. Reuters, 11 Feb. 2013. Web. 12 May 2015.

10. George Weigel. *The End and the Beginning: Pope John Paul II—The Victory of Freedom, the Last Years, the Legacy*. New York: Doubleday, 2010. Print. 384.

11. Ibid. 385.

12. Ibid. 386.

13. George Weigel. *Witness to Hope: The Biography of Pope John Paul II*. Harper, 2001. Print. 680.

14. Neil Ascherson. "John Paul: The Millennial Pope." *Frontline*. PBS, n.d. Web. 12 May 2015.

15. John L. Allen Jr. "Global Priest Shortages, Faith and Reason In the U.K. and a Loss In Ohio." *National Catholic Reporter*. National Catholic Reporter, 9 Dec. 2011. Web. 12 May 2015.

INDEX

Agca, Mehmet Ali, 58–60
Angelicum, 37
anti-Semitism, 19, 27, 64–66, 68

Catholic Church
   and abortion, 72–76
   and contraception, 71, 72–76, 77, 93
   hierarchy of the Catholic Church, 36
   and homosexuality, 77
   sex abuse scandal, 84–87
   and women, 71, 76–79, 93
Clinton, Bill, 75–76
Cold War, 37, 69
College of Cardinals, 7
communism, 36–37, 40–42, 43, 44, 45, 46, 54, 57, 58, 62–63, 64, 67–69, 71, 86, 92
Conclave, 8–10
culture of death, 74

Felici, Senior Cardinal Pericle, 11, 12
Figelwicz, Father, 24, 31

Gdańsk, Poland, 45, 58
Geoghan, John, 84–85
Golden Jubilee, 83–84
Gorbachev, Mikhail, 68–69

Hitler, Adolf, 23, 25, 30
Holocaust, 19, 27, 52, 83

Jagiellonian University, 23, 25, 42
Jaruzelski, General Wojciech, 67, 69
John Paul I, Pope, 7, 8, 47
John Paul II, Pope
   assassination attempt, 58–60
   beatification, 94, 95
   canonization, 94–95
   death, 88
   election, 7–12
   evangelization, 79–81
   funeral, 88–91
   illness, 87–88
   image, 50–53
   inauguration, 49–51
   legacy, 91–95
   on modern issues, 71–81
   travel, 53–55
   vacations, 62
   See also Wojtyla, Karol Jozef, Jr.

Kluger, Jerzy, 19, 52
Kotlarcyzk, Mieczyslaw, 20–21
Kraków, Poland, 15, 21, 23, 24, 26, 31, 32, 38, 40, 43, 47, 52, 68
Królikiewicz, Halina, 26

liberation theology, 54, 62–64

Niegowici, Poland, 38, 50

papal cassocks, 11
papal elections, 10
Parkinson's Disease, 87, 95
Paul VI, Pope, 7, 46, 50
Politi, Marco, 52
Popemobile, 60

Romero, Archbishop Oscar, 61–64

Saint Florian's Church, 40
Saint Peter's Basilica, 7, 8
Saint Peter's Square, 7, 11, 12, 49, 58–60, 61, 83, 88, 90, 94
Sapieha, Adam, 21, 31, 32, 35–36, 40
Second Vatican Council, 43, 50
Sistine Chapel, 8
Solidarity movement, 58, 61, 67–68
Stalin, Joseph, 23, 25, 30, 31, 32

Tyranowski, Jan, 27–28

Vatican, 8, 41, 43, 50, 52, 60, 62, 63, 74, 75, 86, 91, 95
Vatican City, Italy, 7

Wadowice, Poland, 15, 18, 20, 21, 26, 52
Walesa, Lech, 58, 68
Wojtyla, Edmund (brother), 15, 18, 19–20
Wojtyla, Emilia (mother), 15, 16, 20
Wojtyla, Karol, Sr. (father), 15, 16–18, 23, 24, 28–30
Wojtyla, Karol Jozef, Jr.
　archbishop, 43
　cardinal, 43–44
　childhood, 15–21
　early career, 35–44
　education, 23, 25–26, 42
　hobbies, 38
　human rights, 44–46
　ordination, 35–36
　See also John Paul II, Pope
Wojtyla, Olga (sister), 15
World Day of Prayer for Peace, 66
World War II, 23–26, 27, 30–32

111

ABOUT THE AUTHOR

Judy Dodge Cummings is a writer and history teacher from Wisconsin. She has a BA in history and an MFA in creative writing for children and teenagers from Hamline University. As a college student, Judy studied in Europe. On Easter Sunday in 1982, she was among the crowd in Saint Peter's Square when Pope John Paul II delivered the blessing from his balcony.

ABOUT THE CONSULTANT

Dr. Massimo Faggioli is an associate professor of theology at the University of Saint Thomas in Saint Paul, Minnesota. He received his PhD from the University of Turin in Turin, Italy in 2002. He is a researcher, author, and lecturer on such topics as the history of Christianity, the Second Vatican Council, and religion and politics. Faggioli is author of the book, *Vatican II: The Battle for Meaning* (2012), *True Reform: Liturgy and Ecclesiology in Sacrosanctum Concilium* (2012), and *A Council for the Global Church. Receiving Vatican II in History* (2015).